Safe House for Men

A Guide to Better Living

James Mickler

authorHOUSE®

AuthorHouse™
1663 Liberty Drive
Bloomington, IN 47403
www.authorhouse.com
Phone: 1-800-839-8640

First published by AuthorHouse   2/23/2011

ISBN: 978-1-4520-9974-3 (sc)
ISBN: 978-1-4520-9970-5 (e)

Library of Congress Control Number: 2010917429

Printed in the United States of America

Any people depicted in stock imagery provided by Thinkstock are models, and such images are being used for illustrative purposes only. Certain stock imagery © Thinkstock.

This book is printed on acid-free paper.

Table of Contents

DEDICATED
TO
SAYRE GOLDEN MICKLER

"Change, shit! I guess change is good for any of us. What ever it takes for any of ya'll niggas to get up out the hood. Shit! I'm with you, I aint mad at you I aint got nothing but love for you. Do your thing boy...." (Tupac Sharkur All Eyes On Me Tr. 13)

INTRO:

THIS BOOK IS A guide for a better living, amongst the evil that's already inside you. Not knowing who the enemy is, will only hinder you from controlling your well being, and decision making. Why not take back what's rightfully yours and get back your birth rights and the good that every Man can posses. "It doesn't have to be the way they want it to be. You're the only person that should be in your mind, take steps toward becoming a Man. Not knowing is like, not knowing at all. Why not show the world how much power we have, and become King". With the Game everybody has a chance to have the glory of what God wanted from Mankind!(June - The World - And Everything In It)

CHAPTER 1

"KING JAMES
THE RULES TO THE GAME"

*"He who knows not and know not he knows he is a fool.
He who knows not and knows not he is simple teach him.
He who knows and knows not he knows he is a sleep,
awaken him. He who knows and knows that he knows
he is wise follow him."*

(Bruce Lee)

THE GAME HAS NUMEROUS reason to benefit you and who ever that wants to know how to execute or prevent certain things from happening. Not just relationships but other aspects to life that go unexplained and the Game confronts those situation. The education to life lesson are part of the transition to Manhood. History of people, places and spiritual ideas, are little pieces to the puzzle. Relationships and wars has strategies, that need to be defined by any means necessary! Like they say; *"a mind is terrible thing to waste."*

Mind control and seduction, are a pimps tool to a better life. From childhood to adulthood you will be tested by love and temptation, and what will you do? These aspects of life can't be contested, unless you have knowledge of the good and the bad things that take place in the world. That's why life is for learning and anybody that's not learning, won't understand the Game! See information has to be sought after, that's real education. Not to be boxed into somebody else's dream! A long time ago, people use to travel thousand of miles to listen or conversant with a wise old Man and the teaching or Game that they would receive would help them in their quest for knowledge. The power that you will posses will be the will power or actually thinking with your brain, and it won't be any wrong answers. Only studying and zero tolerance to opposing enemies, will leave you in a position of control. Your life is determine by a positive and a negative action that you allow into your existent . Throughout history Man has taught their sons this Game. However, gaps of knowledge led to the feminist movement and so many Men have taken a back seat to the bitch! Leaving the Women alone and confused. See the Game provides constellation of stars that provide information to a better life. A new way at looking at yourself without even looking. Now that's Game! So with every move you make you must in great hast do what is ask of you. To do so puts you inside the script that we at Safe House called the Game! Many honorable Men got left behind not paying attention to what lies before them. The art of anything provide answers to question needed in your path to the Game. So without moving, will leave your position in your house hold in question. But with the birds and the wind and a clear mind the next step is a step towards greatness. So position yourself in a chess board manner and take advantage of your enemy surroundings and the Game will reveal its self as a part of life. The Game is what a pimp likes to call protection against all life form that attack. (Like a immune system) The seven sense that provides you with knowledge of thinking ahead before taking action is based on right, verse wrong theory. This gift is only used when thing don't make sense, rather if it due to a relationship or a confrontation. What ever the situation is, the Game can't tolerate an evil Purpose. Remember the sky is watching and life is to short to make the wrong move. However in today's world, people are brain washed and have no purpose! So at Safe House we offer the strategies that will lead you to the Game. It's hard to walk the tight rope of life without the right teaching and its, even harder not to believe in oneself. However, the Game, (the weapon of choice) has rules to follow while in engaging in conflict with the enemy. The King James version of the Game is only helpful with knowledge of logical thinking. To be able to decipher codes of bullshit, will help in your journey through life, without that gift your standing in a war zone with no weapons. The choice to have rules when dealing with the opposition, will only make your Kingdom run smoothly, and the mind has to be rested when dealing with such matters. The rules to the Game, is to put rules in place, so the enemy will have boundaries when dealing with your Manhood!

CHAPTER 2

"THE MIND"

THE MIND IS SOMETHING you shouldn't waste. So why let your mind hinder you from making the right decision. In God good book we are told that there is a foundation to a family:

(A) A Father
(B) A Mother
(C) A Child

As you can see the father is first and the mother is second and last but not least the child. But that doesn't mean that the father and the mother isn't equal in the relationship, we just have different jobs to do. The

Woman has things to do like nurturing and the Man has things to do like providing. That's why Women are created to be helpmeets and you the leader, and the child is left, being the heir to the thrown. How would it play out if your son or daughter sees the confusion that's in the relationship? Father and potential fathers take back your Kingdom. Don't let your heir see the mass destruction that being pushed by the powers to be. To be first or second it really doesn't matter, what really matters is only third. But, I know people our trying to figure out what first means! Does it mean control the other person? No, because we control each other, so that cant be. Lets me explain and try to pay attention, lets go to the King James Bible: When Abraham told his wife that was his half sister, when he got close to Egypt, that he said to Sara his wife;

"Indeed I know you are a Woman of beautiful and confidence therefore it will happen when the Egyptians see you that they will kill me but they will let you live. So God told him to tell his wife that as the Egyptians is near that I am your brother rather than your husband and that they will let me live."(Abraham- King James Bible)

In doing that and being a good wife and going against the head people at that time, God granted her children at an old age. Abraham gave his wife awareness of a foundation of a family. Sara listened to God voice that came out of Abraham mouth and delivered like she was created for. Then came the child by the name of Isaac. See how the relationship developed, if she played her role and Abraham played his, then God granted them a seed. The mind has to be able to move like the wind! It can't be defeated at any cost! We as Men, have to be defined. But to do so one would of have had direct contact with one. The Webster definition to the word Man is human being an adult male the human race Mankind one possessing in high degree the qualities considered distinctive of Manhood an adult male servant or employee the individual who can fulfill one requirements one of the pieces with which various Games like chess and also one of the players on a team often cap white society or people. Now, here at Safe House we claim the definition of Man to be is, Human race a soldier or a warrior a real male person by an act a pimp a King a male person who knows oneself the individual who can fulfill ones requirements as Man. We forget that God created Man to populate his surroundings with children that will either be boy or girl an eventually Man and Woman. So how you rule as Man effect every body in the foundation. The schooling that you bring in to your home can't be elementary, it has to be mindful of the families growth. There can't be any none sense or foolishness when it comes to your life, because the people in your castle need your support. You have to make the right decisions your life depends on it. Your family depends on it! The Samurai live by a code, and that code exist in the harts of Men. So why do we lack the discipline and the knowledge we need to begin life? Why does the mind choose not to accept the code or the Game? Life is the opposite of death and we choose death over life, because its easier to take that path when life doesn't make sense. At an early age we as human beings find reason to be depended on others, instead of relying on ones inner self. The systematic slavery control your life and other people find ways of leading you into something that will destroy your purpose for being here! And life not that simple by any means. However if you keep choosing the wrong path than your already dead. The code of Man comes from the inside, it doesn't matter how many children you have and its not how good you can fight. It comes from wisdom and experience. The stuff that make Men real! Man have always beckon on tradition, the same on old bull crap. That's not life, life is meant for growth like the rose that grows through the concrete. See in the Game the mind functions to protect its well being, meaning the wealth of his Kingdom and the family. But humanity has already chosen death scared of what people might say, frantic that he or she might leave. Its sick not to know one's boundaries or limits. How is it that the Game that you present to the world is weak? Take time to live and pay attention to the Game, and always think logical when dealing with others. The pimp is always watching and he ready for you to make a mistake that can cause you your soul. Take responsibilities for the things you do! The children need your help and also the Woman, you create the respect that they richly deserve. The ideal Woman knows this, that's why she gives us a hard time. See if you perform the duties that are ask of you than the Woman is already yours. It's the living sprit in you that makes the Game possible. So why not take the high road when it comes to your life, because you might not live a long one. The picture I present to you is full of colors and full of stories, that with the help of the Game you should advance in the life. However, your mind has to have the perception of what is most important to you. Your family and the Kingdom or the path that will lead you to failure.

" *So what is it gona be? You'll gona be the pimp or the pimpy, the player or the one that gets played. Your gona get fucked or your gona get laid…!"(Goldie The Griot From Tela Track 18)*

CHAPTER 3

"REAL PEOPLE DO REAL THINGS"

Real Men stand tall in the face of knowledge! But, to be real one will have to walk in the foot steps of legends to be only tested in the knowledge of the old". (June- Real Men - The World And Everything In It)

Take a picture or look in the mirror and ask yourself, do I like the person I see? If u can't answer your own question than your already defeated. The first step in knowing one self is to find your own common ground. People leave the door open to bullshit, so their reality doesn't have a peace mind. The life you choose, has an impact on your situation, as being who you are! How can anyone not take their life serious, when you know your purpose! Why choose to listen to the bullshit, when you don't have to? The enemy shouldn't be in your circle anyway. Once they brake down your circle and enter your life without permission, than they show that their life is meaningless. Anybody that puts so much of their time in your life has problems of their own. And how can anybody with problems enter your circle. The first step in knowing oneself should come from the inside not from other people. Self-worth comes from the middle of the heart, and if you don't have that than you don't have self-esteem. To enter your dragon, you have to have courage, and you have to prepare for a battle that confronts you on all sides. To do this, you have to know who you are and who you are becoming! This book is a gift to true believers of the Game. Not for the weak individual that doesn't want the Game! Through out this book, Game will be discussed on levels comparable to Kings. Being real to yourself is like knowing oneself and half of the Men in the world don't try to find oneself. That's why Men are playing out position, right in the hands of his true enemy. However, time and time again people try to understand what real means. Not every Man in origin knows how to be real. But the Game needs real individuals to take part in to a means to a end to this systemize slavery. Why is it, that people tend to play themselves, when it comes to their lives.

Day after day, they defy their God and take their lives for a rollercoaster ride to hell and back, just to do it again and again until they reach rock bottom? Back in the days when real Men roamed the earth, it wasn't any mystery on what a Man was, and now this! What happen to the Soldiers and the Philosopher, that taught this part of the Game? Where are the real Men that put the growth of his children first instead of a bitch that doesn't mean him or the child any good? It was told to me that we as human beings only use a portion of our brains, that's why the Game is so important because slavery is so broad that it has no end. However, real people understand the Game because inside them lies a pimp waiting for a chance to get paid! To be a Man is wonderful thing, it is what God created only imperfect because of greed. The first chance at the tree of knowledge and he didn't act real enough to get more chances at the truth! See after the curse, God still gave Man chances, but for century Man been sick with not knowing who they our. Now why is it so hard to fix what's broken? Its impossible to move your army or your family to what is progress if your stuck at the basics. Life is for learning, if you go through life without fixing what's wrong than your life not worth living. The point for creation is to grow, but if your child knows more than you how can he or she exceed at a better life than the one you accomplish! Why, fathom that type of life when the Game can save your house hold. Like I said, to be real is to know oneself or to know who he going to be. The difference in today's world, the generation has no teachers, they're the students to the Game getting taught like robots in a program that repeats its self over and over, like a answering machine. Being real has its perks, for one you will seek greatness from oneself. For two you'll get to see the growth inside your family and hey, maybe the world! See, I think that real people do real things, like a King watching over his Kingdom waiting and watching for enemies to attack. If you as Man can't keep your head in the Game and be as real as possible than you will be exile from your thrown. The Game supports the theory that in war, the one called Man should, take up arms and defend his lands. But to be real one should already be armed and ready for anything! Your life, is your life. How you govern your body, controls your circle. The family need your Manhood, so they will have something to believe in. To live a life without structure, is a life that is doomed.

CHAPTER 4

"THE WORLD AND EVERYTHING IN IT"

"SAFE HOUSE BRINGS YOU to a world, that tells the mind, that war is around the corner! The battle can't hinder you from taking control your life. If you choose to except profit instead of losses, than the battle is already won. But the one who chooses to dwell in affairs that will lead him to failure is a fool! See the Game to put yourself into in position to be able to place yourself into a different light rather than the same old darkness, will only make things better in the long run. If you choose to disobey the Game and remain the same and not evolve, than your situation is in great danger. People who don't want more and choose to take the road of no return will never reach adulthood. To be total Man, is to reach as far as possible so you can adapt to what the world has place in front of you!"

General! Put your last name first when dealing with worldly people. While marching into the sun set, step with left foot first. Present the next level of the Game. Show Safe House method of being a Man, A soldier, a General! The world is filled with bitches, with hopes of destroying your mind frame. The tactical methods of being open minded to the situation, will only haunt the other individuals one sided way of thinking. A General runs his outfit. He plans his strategies, so he can remain on earth at least another day! Demand progress from oneself. To believe in any other way of thinking will put you on other side of the battle field. The chess board manner is needed to understand what war means. At Safe House, the General commands his forces and train his Men and his Women to become productive soldiers. But before you train anybody. your mind should have plain for one self to becoming a Man.

"Life is a Game of inches. You move up little by little till the fame and riches. Life gives you Game and a broad of vision. Some niggas is hoes and all women ain't

bitches…!" (Eight ball - From Pimp C Greatest hits Track 19)

General, stop what you doing. Revise the plain. Safe House demands the truth! Your life is in jeopardy, and you don't even know it. Always be armed. The enemy wants you not to evolve. They want you to be defenseless, helpless and confused of the truth. It's better to be aware, rather than being fooled in believe not to be! Where does that leave you? Who will lead your army? Or will an early death be your purpose? How you control your well being, determines your money making and your love making. The situation in getting money or in better terms getting what is owe to you, will only finance your production in building your dynasty. Stop the reoccurrence of failure and strive to be General, in this world that is always at war! To penetrate the Game, you should always remember that war is always on the horizon. How you govern your body Shows you how to move in the Game. The truth will even set a convict free! So failure is not an option, not at all!

"Seriously listen to me, your attention give it to me. Ya'll niggas ready for it? Revolution prove it to me. Stand tall man up, if your scared go home. This shit here ain't temporarily, this shit here life long…!(Eight Ball - Set up Shop Track 6)

To be General one has to see the control that he has over himself , so he can see the bullshit that's been place in front of his feet. Remember without thinking you can't move your feet! So always think in the manner of what is profitable for you and your family. The Game support the idea that survival is a Man best friend, when dealing with life. Safe house, needs Generals to have the mind set of " *Forward March,*" so he can deliver the messages to their feet. To be out of money and out on the street is not what we at Safe House prescribes to its followers. Successes should be on your mind while leading your army into battle. Man up and present total Man to a population of adversaries trying to over throw your position! The conspiracy to destroy Man, leaves you to shift yourself into high gear and put a strategy together to conquer your fear and your dreams. A General demands the truth! " *That's mind over bitches* " (June - The world and everything in it)

The world and everything in it, is suppose to be you're God giving right. However, the negative energy is pointed in your direction, leaving the gates to your city wide open for unwanted visitors. The bitch was sent by the King of the masses to deflect your positive energy, causing confusion in the balance in the human make up! To many problems in the world not enough time, should be a thought that's on the mind.

"You win battles by knowing the enemy's timing, and using a timing which the enemy does not expect."(Miyamoto Musashi 1584-1645)

To be or not to be is the answer! The bitch is the question in the manner of which we are speaking. The Game in the answer leaves people to believe in a choice! Choices, to accompany or tolerate the question of bitch, puts your well being in great danger. Your mind needs to decipher friend or foe before any type of relationship takes place. M.O.B puts you in the driving seat towards the separation that is needed from the bitch! To pursue a profitable life, comes with obstacles. Male and female predators find ways to make their lives yours. Always put a stamp on what you want! The character of the individual demands the truth. And the truth is that the world is based on a money system, which puts you into a column that's either for profit or for losses Where does that put yourself when it comes to your life? Do you believe that the world want you to fail, or do you believe that you want yourself to fail? While marching into the sun set, the Game will provide shelter from the idea of failure. The world and everything in it, gives you the right to, *"Evaluate the one you call friends"*

(Randi Blackmon) so where does that leave you now? Safe House takes you to a place where your mind should put unimportant things that you hold dear to the side to focus on one thing at a time! However, complete the task at hand or you will be consume by the bullshit! Remember that the things you hold dear will come if you keep pushing, but without following the direction that you plan for yourself, will only put you in a place where your not moving at all. The truth is that the bitch wants to throw you off track, to something that seems profitable but later will only end in defeat. The right decision is only your decision to make! Take control your position and make the right adjustments to rise up out the gutter. Remember that hell is always waiting for you turn around. So stop looking around for some one to give you a hand. Take a look at oneself. Make the mind see the bitch that's been placed in your path. Know that your situation is based on your performance in the maze of life. So what you put into life, is how you get out the maze! Safe House gives you a escape route out of the maze that's control your mind. Participation in the rescue of ones sanity, will help with the understanding of oneself. To jump outside oneself to notice the conflict, explains a lot about who you are and how you handle the problem. However, bitches tend to brake their word, for some type of gain! So trust will always be a factor. The Game to figure out the bitch, Should be replayed over and over again. Total concentration on words that's being presented to you, will open up gaps of bad intention. So where does that leave you? Money leaves space in between those gaps. However, the bitch clogs up the middle and leaves it hard to be productive in today's society. A case of M.O.B will direct you to a road of choice. That road should lead you towards being in this world and getting everything you want out of it. Always keep the eye on the prize, when walking in the steps of another. This will only damage your chance of recognizing your self sprit. The *"Game"* is believed to be uplifting in these time. Look at yourself and ask yourself, will I let another influence my way of thinking. Help yourself achieve success in a way that people wouldn't think of you! War is all day and all night. The state of mind should see the bad intention before the conversation is over. Remember, don't let anything stop your cash flow. The reason for this, is because bills still have to get paid and children still have to eat. It's unthinkable not to create a picture of your future. To be lost in the transaction and not place yourself in the Game will stop you from earning your way. To be broke and not to appreciate life itself, is a hole that's deeper than you can image. So why not put your well being in front of the bitch! To hate yourself, for placing this animal into your thought process will only correct your vision. Your seeing in a another demension, confused to not think logical, when it comes to your own survival. At Safe House, we recognize the bitch as anything that move against you and your family. The fear of becoming a better person leaves you in a field of dreams. To be Man, is to be a provider! The castle needs your ambition to brake the cycle of failure. But, if you don't have ambition to make it to a better place in your life, than your mind has already shut down. Depression chooses the individual that it hangs on to. It's your choice to accept the harassment or not. Your life means something, even though your enemies will show disrespect when it comes to your mindset! So depression shouldn't shut down your system, it at some point should feel like pain, causing some type of movement. The bitch loves the idea that depression is on the mind. As long as it is being discussed, the longer it takes to brake the hold! The Game to see the bitch takes the abilities, known only to Men that can see with the Third Eye! Safe House Commands the army to move in the direction of victory. The bitch see's your flaws and wants to flirt with your human nature. To separate your situation from the bitch puts the bitch in their own little place. The belief system in yourself creates an opportunity to be successful, but to be weak and not commit to the Game is like hanging on to some type failure. Move in the direction of high ground when dealing with flood season, because bullshit is on it way. My hope is that you see their Game, before they see yours! Remember what was took from you, then ask yourself; how can I retrieve back my mind, soul, desire, ambition and any other properties that make up who you are? Don't let anything thing get in between you and your plan. The mind should be military when setting up operation. Your position is to be defended at all cost. The enemy waits and watches to see your everyday paterens, so they can expose themselves to you and your family. Safe House delivers the code to Man in a formula, of family first and bullshit last. The proection of the *"State"* makes all enemies question warfare. A Kingdom that thinks together builds a stronger offspring! So The world and everything in it, should be a quest for only people who want to improve themselves from being at a stand still, or to someone who's making moves! Don't be bullied into believing that nothing is better than something. Getting paid or being broke, take your pick, but remember that the real wealth is in knowledge of old. My friend, it takes the hustle of a pimp to create the Game necessary to free yourself from a world filled with bitches and hoes! Where does that leave you now? Picture yourself controlling your life, and not what's been orcastraighted to you on behalf of the King of the masses. His plans for you is slavery or death, which won't bring you any profit. Your plan for yourself, should be to get in and get out. No matter how you retrive your currency, remember to use your head when dealing with your soul, because

James Mickler

the bitch is on the prowl and their mission is to decive
and destroy you!

CHAPTER 5

"ENERGY"

GOOD OR BAD ENERGY, as long as you have energy! This is important because women are attracted to it. They crave it, it like the sun staring right at them making them feel warm inside. There are so many different levels of energy, some people who's over confident have amazing energy and people see them as a threat. Others have low levels and are seen as nobodies. I was talking to this woman the other day and she came to me with this story. It's seemed her friend was dating a guy who was over confident of what he had. He worked two jobs and he had his own apartment. Her complaint was that he didn't have to act like he had more than every other guy.

She felt like, there was more out there than he had seen. This poor guy was dating a person who had a potential to be a bitch. (See at Safe House we show you what not to date.) Rather than provide this guy with Godly energy that he needed, she broke him down in her mind to what she thought he would become. How can you take a Man that's working two job and think in a manner that he thinks he better than every one else? In his defense, he deserve to be treated as a hero amongst his peers, not because he worked two jobs. But, because he stands tall while in the mist of a bunch of monsters! The energy that she showed only puts a damper on her retrieving what she wanted. If this is a good guy she shouldn't worry about how confident he was about his situation, she should be showing him the energy and courtesy that a Man deserve. Why would anyone knock this Man down, when he doing what other so called Men, are not doing? A Woman supposed to support him, not to take all his energy from him. What will she gain from killing this Man with negative energy? Leverage, another form of energy that this potential bitch was using, has no meaning in any situation because if that Man has no rights than, that Woman has none either. Bitches use leverage as a form of bad energy to control a part of the relationship. For some odd reason her temptation to were the pants in the house hold, has her missing the boat, if I may say! Her lack of supporting energy has her in war against her mate. She should use less energy on her mate and more on her goals in life. When you have connecting energy in a relationship, everything is better. The conversation , the sex and the mindset. Why should each individual be on a different level when dealing with each other? So why not please yourself and use corrective energy so you and your mate can live in perfect harmony!

Confidence is another form of energy. Your self-esteem should be at a great high. How can you lead if you don't have the confidence to do so? The showmanship of walking with your head high will only lead you to being under attack. People seem to hate others when their confidence is on the horizon. It's like being the King of the jungle or being the guy with so much class, that Women can't refuse. Take yourself out of your mind, and realize the power your Man energy or swag, that you possesses. Nobody should be able to duplicate who you are. You're the only person who walks like you and talks like you. Your swag is your pimp and your pimp is your Manhood. They can't duplicate who you are if you don't change your mind and try being something that your not! That's why you see people out in the world looking like robots, emotionless with blank faces and doing what everybody else is doing! Confidence is a big part of who you are, its tied to the dating scene as the first thing a human being notice when putting their eyes upon your shell, that holds your energy! Remember it's what's on the inside that shows what's on the outside. Like I said early, some people have a lot of energy and some have nothing to live for. Men, be what you are and show your Man powers. Tell the world that in your own little way to gaze at me and take a picture! Rock your life like you have a million dollars, just so they can see you perform. It's your television show and people want to see if you're going to fail or to see you accomplish what you were created for! Last but not least seduction, Seduction is the main component in the energy factor without it your just human without the being; *"The art of seduction is designed to arm you with weapons of persuasion and charm, so that those around you will slowly lose their ability to resist without knowing how or why it has happened. It is an art of war for delicates times."*(Robert Green)

This quote by Robert Green, brought myself meaning to the word energy. All through history Man and Woman used seduction to trap or free each other. There was Cleopatra the Queen of Egypt who seduce great Kings with her beauty. There was also Casanova who brought Women pleasure with the Game that came from his mouth, and swag that showed from his attire. Now both of theses persons, had high levels of energy and it showed through their use of seduction.

And lets not for get King Solomon who use the power of his songs and poems to seduce the dark skin bride! Like I said, this Game that Safe House present can be comparable to Kings. If you choose to be seductive than you choose to use energy that can't be used for a negative purpose, if so than you yourself will lose. A pimps powers of seduction can only be manifested with good intention, not to trick or abuse the person of choice. There are people who take this form of energy and run with it. But, with my knowledge of the Game, and seeing people like Tiger Woods destroying his self pride and his family just because he couldn't govern his self or control his energy, makes me think the Game is very important to today's youth when dealing with fragile harts. We as adults have to teach this part of the Game with good intention. Our Women and are children need direction so they won't become something we as a generation will fear!

"Safe House believes, that the Man is needed to lead the people to some kind of energy source. Without Man, the people would wonder the desert for 40 years or more." (With Out Man - Safe House)

CHAPTER 6

"SEPERATION" BY MONEY

MONEY SHOULDN'T HAVE ANY air time in your relationship. However, it finds its way to be more damaging than cheating on your spouse. Why is money so effective in ruing a relationship? We as Men are commanded in one way or another to regulate our funds to please Women. I was driving the other day when I came across a build board on the side of a bus that stated, *"What she wants!"* And on the other side it said; *"Diamonds are forever!"* What I got from this ad, that if your love is for sure, than buy this three to four carrot diamond for the Woman that stands next to you! Now I don't see anything wrong with a Man that spends money on a Woman. But not a bitch! If that Woman doesn't work for it, she doesn't deserve to be dress down in jewels like the Queen of Sheba! Like I presented Queen! A Queen works for her King and her subjects! She supposed to serve the people. If I am Man, and I take initiative to spend my hard earn money on you, than you as a Woman is going to put in more from the beginning, while I will give in from the start! See, I see things different. I don't put anyone on a pedestal and I don't think Men that's trying to get to know somebody should put so much effort in the money department because, if he decide to marry, that Woman than he'll probably spend more money than he would choose! That's children, marriage, divorce, and separation and also alimony and maybe even if your lucky child support can be taken out of your pay check! Take a look at your circumstance. If you choose to keep abusing yourself, by letting money control your relationships than you are already in one of these situation. The Woman has to show her true colors and only a Woman will show her true colors! But if she is Woman than treat her with the respect of a Queen. Safe House can only be described in logic. If that Woman in origin would have you spend all your money on her and she didn't offer to lend a helping hand than its probably a bitch, trying to separate you from your money. My logical way of thinking makes me believe that this person is taking advantage of your character. Real Man and real Women don't take advantage of each other. See a pimp that's see a potential prostitute, can't help but to conquer her, That's what Men do! Check your history. Through out history Great Kings or Pharaohs conquer other countries by means of pimping. The reason for the history lesson is to show you, that you have to know the past to have a chance at a future. Money is to hard to come by, that's why your mind has to be focused on the person not the camouflage. Don't get caught in the trap, when your either getting robed or getting Man trained.! The bitch doesn't have a hart. Some times we get caught up loving while they're lusting or the other way around. The point in this, is that money gives off a illusion an American dream! Is that dream for you? Give up your money and get nothing in return. That's not King like! Look at what you want out of life. Everybody should know I'm an individual and person to person should apply to all situation. Ask the lady next to you, if she would lend you some money, when you just got together! That's what you're doing! I'm not saying don't. But don't get caught in the camouflage! The principalities in your affairs should be protected, and not lend out to a possible individual who's not for you. Money by separation or separate your money from the situation! The people you have in your life have to know this from the beginning! They have to be taught something about you. Your explanation for your behavior should explain your zero tolerance clause in your contract. Because no mean no! Don't let this monster control your pre dating methods with a old way of thinking. The reason being, a lot things have changed. The Women of today are being control by the bitch. The population control of the Woman in today society are a means of destroying the Man as we know it. The bitch has confused the so called Man to once again to steel from the tree of knowledge. Real Men obey the truth, and don't let a person of interest, train his mind to believe otherwise. Your position in your house, (that's your well being) should be to control the situation from the beginning. Life in the money department has to be watch and maintain. The Game has to be planed and played over and over again. Not just with the bitch, but also with family and friends. Safe House demands the truth! People who defy the Game also defy themselves by not believing in oneself. I had this family member who had one agenda and I had another. He owed me some money and his agenda was to pay me when he chosen too. My thoughts about this family member before the situation, was cool! However, with the vision to see the bullshit my thoughts about him has change. Money by separation should have been in play. My choice and his agenda, to run the show, put the family in a blind spot and sacrifice the loyalty that I had for him. The root to all evil can destroy Kingdoms! Its your job to isolate your center, (that's your core) from outside influences. People tend to be led astray from the Game by individuals who appear to be dishonest from the beginning. To separate lies from reality takes the knowledge of 48 laws of power!. The vision has to have a open mind to an motive that will lead you to believe that you should make it rain to impress some one who you want for free or someone you want to help on their feet. Money in all situation can't get caught up in something that holds no value! A Man without knowledge, is not a Man. He is just a child pretending to be one!

CHAPTER 7

"DECEPTION"

"Governments saw Men in mass; but our Men, being irregulars, were not formations, but individuals... Our Kingdom lay in each Man's mind."(Seven Pillars Of Wisdom. T E Law 1883-1935)

M OST OF WHAT MEN know or been train to know is a lie! Education and the use of the third eye will bring your enemy Down to what is know as planet earth. Space is a black hole that never stops. It's so dark and so big that it is deceiving to the eye's;

"The Third Eye of the Spy. In the land of the two- eyed, the third eye gives you omniscience of god . You see further

than others, and you see deeper into them. Nobody safe from the eye but you."(Image - 48 Laws Of Power)

The space between words, leave room for lies. It's your own fault if you find yourself trapped in that black hole. What the mind chooses to believe is what the eyes finds confusing. Society, doesn't present a clear picture to you and your family! The picture, suggest deception is a method in confusing the watcher to see things as the King of the masses see's them. People tend to see things not for themselves but, through other people eye's. For example how can anybody witness anything if he or she wasn't there, and how can anybody let others dictate their perception? The power of hypnosis on the individuals, takes the understanding of the mind. Rather, than play back the situation before the situation takes place, you decide to put yourself in a compromising position, and since you were already weak from the mental abuse, the spell has taken over your brain, making you lose all logic and even your identity! Deception is used through out the day by people who want something for nothing! However, at Safe House we speak of honesty when it comes to a Man's word. My hopes with help of the Game, that you decipher the Earth's code, so Man can live free from the bullshit. Power and greed awaken the bitch, leaving their deception in the air. Braking down, moments in life gives you a better picture of a negative situation, placing the mind at ease;

"Men are so simple of mind, and so much dominated by their immediate needs, that a deceitful Man will always find plenty who are ready to be deceived." (Niccolo' Machiavelli 1469-1527 48 Laws Of Power)

The King of the masses, wants you to be under his spell for control. To persuade, a people to believe that they need to be judge was genius! The Game suggest ownership of one's soul. To only be judge by God! Where does that leave you? Your mind can't be confused to believe that the King of the masses wants you to know the truth. Do you believe in truth? Or are you the deceived, that he trick with his trickery! Then I ask the questions again; how can someone let another dictate their perception? And how can anybody witness anything if he or she was not there? Deception brings forth darkness over the mind, controlling the body to react in harmony with negative energy. Place yourself in the shoes of another, to witness the abuse that could happen to you! The Game offers you a way to brake the bitches plot of controlling your psychic. But, only Man can reach this goal of Space Age thinking! The deception that everything is equal isn't smoke, but a fire that's been burning since the beginning. To see truth for what it is or to set a stander for the bullshit that you choose to accompany. *"A mind is a terrible thing to waste."* See the Game to use your Third Eye will help you to see deeper into that individual. In society the people don't use their heads when it comes to what they think. They only do what they are told. To brake a Man, change his perception of who he is, and he will not know anything! Deception can be used in many forms. For example; How did half of the world, have the same opinion about Mr. OJ Simpson, and how did this hate for this Man get out of control? The people who choose to have hate for this Man, have been blinded by the imagination of words that been presented to them. The Game issue a warning to the individual who believes in hate crimes. To the one that hates for a reason, your destiny will leave you without a cause! Trapped into the maze looking for reason for being here. However, if it wasn't for his lawyer knowing the Game and knowing how to play it, he would of went to jail for murder! But the law is filled with deception, the hate for this Man followed him until he ran out of time in Las Vegas. Stress and fatigue, killed the image of Mr. Simpson. The brake down, from actually winning the case and still losing his swag, left him in a room full of enemies. And since he was already labeled a monster, it didn't matter if he did it or not! From 1992 to 2009, this Man has been tracked and hunted. The deception in this example was to get the people to look into the television and witness the bullshit. The people didn't get the facts, because the police had their hands full with planting evidence and contaminating the crime scene. So the people were caught up into somebody else's hate. It's sick not to read between the lines and to take, other people advice about someone else. The King of the masses has help wanted signs for the mindless soul, so the Elite will have their thoughts. To control the masses, you have to have the attention of a people who needs to be saved, so the bitch can unleash their deception upon them! So in Mr. Simpson case, he was guilty in the minds of the public and not bye the court. The court and the media presented the bullshit to the public, letting people help judge this Man even though nobody really witness anything! The public choose to lean in the favor of the of the situation. The system is design to confuse the mind and the hearts of his victims. The black magic has taken advantage of people minds, making them see things without even looking! Deception is a bitches tool to quickly break the psychic, from a logical way of thinking. At Safe House, you'll learn how to defuse the situation with knowledge of the Game. So to think with a logical way of thinking, will set you free from lies that the King of the masses support on a every day bases. To believe in things without substance will make you a fool! To understand how much power and control these bitches have over you, will take a sharp mind.

Decipher what is real to what is fake, so you will have a chance to see the deception for what it really is. The Game demands it!

" There is much to be known. Life is short, and life is not Life without knowledge. It is therefore an excellent device to acquire knowledge from everybody, thus by the sweat of another's brow, you win the reputation as an oracle."
(Baltasar Gracian, 1601-1658)

CHAPTER 8

"THE BITCH"

"The Woman who can be easily won over to congress:… a Woman who looks sideways at you;…a Woman who hates her husband, or who is hated by him;… a Woman who has not had any children;… a Woman who is very found of society; a Woman who is apparently very affectionate toward her husband; the wife of an actor, a widow;… a Woman found of enjoyments; a vain Woman; a Woman who husband is inferior to her in rank or ability; a Woman who is proud of the arts;… a Woman is slighted without any cause; … a Woman who husband is devoted to traveling; the wife of a jeweler; a jealous Woman; a covetous Woman.(- The Hindu, The Art Of Love Edited By Edward Windsor From The Art Of Seduction.")

Here at Safe House we offer asylum from the animal know as bitch. The word speak for its self. You heard your mother or your father say it, one time or another in reference to a bad human being. Or just when they're mad at something. The Game in this section is better know as discernment. To come to know or recognize and detect with the eyes and mentally defuse the camouflage. The Webster dictionary defines the word or saying bitch to be a female canine: A female dog: A malicious, spiteful, and domineering Woman that likes to complain. Like I said the word describe its self. Now in Safe House the book of dreams, the bitch is, what Woman don't see that's stopping them from getting what they richly deserve. They don't see the danger in accompany this monster or being enslaved by this creature. Man can also be bitches as well, that's why the gift of discernment is available in the Games method in digesting this crooked human being. The vision needed to tell the Woman and the bitch apart is to use common sense. Know in your mind that, a Woman can't really tolerate a bitch and a bitch doesn't want anything to do with a Woman. But in groups they well never turn their backs on their sister, no matter if it's a complete lie! No matter if its Man or Woman or bitch or dog, we have to change are thinking. The things that a bitch can do to you and your family will cost you everything. To see through the thick layer of smoke and mirrors one would of had to have notice signs of abuse. A true person that's wants something out of themselves wants their partner to want the same thing. So why kill the relationship, with being a bitch and ruining the connecting energy that you need. A individual who bring drama into the relationship and means to do so is probably that monster. A person that cares for nothing and always complaining is a potential bitch. It is so many form to this computer program that attacks the nervous system of people, that choose not to live logical. They put themselves in the matrix's where everybody is the same rude and hateful, young and stupid, old and not much better at copying each other. Our Women are few and our Men are dying. The bitch has the world by the balls and no child can lead her! The reason for this transformation is genetic right down to the computer that holds the disk! Watch their sexual habits. If they are over sex and crazed, it's a bitch. They mean you no good, they dress like whores and represent what a Woman will not be! You can spot these bitches, with tight outfits, hair weaved downed and also they choose to be product of main stream media. Not who they were suppose to be, just parasites spreading a awful disease of lies and confusion. Always complaining and saying things like *"I don't need a Man!"* How in the world will they get the chances to receive what they really want. See they lie, and they know with out Man there's no structure. But who has time to wait for their dream to become reality. Your position from the beginning should be honest in what moves needs to be made and the counter part has choices and decisions to make so they can see what street to navigate through. *"He who is honest shall walk with pride and confidence. But if he lies , he shall hold his head in shame."*(Nigotree Barbra Monday)

The domination by this so called Women has confuse the hunter and made him the hunted. Safe House represents the Game at a high degree! Check what's really good for you and see if you can afford this picture of your imagination into your mind or your home! Everything that looks good is not right for your situation.

"A bitch comes a dime a dozen!" (Too Short- Gangster & Strippers Track 8) So why fall for the enemy? How can the hunter get hunted? The art of war that surround your compound has broken down your defenses. The perpetrator has breached your anatomy and is preparing to consume you! The Game that you posses has to prepare you from attacks from the enemy. Your life depends on it. Have you seen the movies lately its program for you to do things you do! (Like who you have in your life) The bitch will agree to disagree for some false profit. She will stir up trouble soon, as she thinks of some selfish needs. Her plains will grow

until you leave without a trace. Her 20 to 45 year rein, will end up in complete denial of the truth and that she is killing our soldiers and leading Mankind into the fantasy land, were Men can be bitches two! The Game that you follow can't be contested, it can't go against what's best for the Kingdom. To do so is like a life style that could be dangerous by means of mind control, sex addition, lust, body pollution , and also wars with other individual and all of these can lead to the down fall of your sprit. My hopes that with the help of Safe House backing you, the Woman that has been place on earth for you is findable. The programmed bitch has had her eyes on you from day one! So the gift of discernment is really important. The Game doesn't have to be one way. It can choose to be what ever way you want it to be. The disguises that this Woman in origin will posses will have demon like ability to maneuver into your Kingdom and break your family and your income. Their objective is to take your family structure and manipulate the blue print that was created for you! Once your out of the garden its hell getting back. You know what I mean? The temptation to have a bitch has you blinded by truth. Woman don't need, hair weaves and tight outfits to present who they are! Can't you see that this is being used to stop you from finding the star that can help put your Kingdom together? Don't get me wrong a Woman that's classy about who she is and puts herself first, before a male bitch is a Woman that is worthy for my Kingdom. The Game only enhances the vision into seeing what's good or bad for you! This bad mouth, trained Man killer gets away with her action by programming damage Woman and Men into a life that's out of position. So Men, your life has to be put together like a puzzle, until every piece is put in its place. The Woman you choose to have, can't be a back stabber that will turn on you for a another Man. How much time do you think you got! Your pimp shouldn't be fazed by the bitch, your Game has to recognized her moves so you can counter her claims to your castle. Be different, don't be the same as the next guy. Hold your ground and sleep with one eye open. Investigate your suppose to be Queen with the Game and conquer the bitch before she terrorized your Kingdom.

CHAPTER 9

"LOVE &THINKING LOGICAL"

"[Is it] better to be loved than feared or feared than loved? It may be answered that one would wish to be both, but, because it is difficult to unite them in one person, it is much safer to be feared than loved." (- Niccolo Machiavelli- The Prince)

L IFE IS NOT SIMPLE at all and love is un logical but, with logic you can recognize its faults, and its beauty's. Sweet love can be tempting and confusing coming from the naked eye. But to be on top of your Game and to be mindful of the fears of not having and wanting love than your Game can be complete! Not without logic can you posses the seductions of the

Game and to use it in a way of tempting the beast, that we call love! Men, we are granted love from the most high, and that high can only be determine by faith. So why do you choose to accept the fear that's been put upon you? Your position in this matter has to come in the form of a leader! If your Kingdom fails than your not ready for Safe House measures of a Man! People get drawn into living a lie instead of living life. How can a Man refuse what God has put in his presence, and how can a so called Man fear his divine gift from the havens above? To do so, doesn't give you good grace with the father God, it only puts you in the dog house. So how can you approach life without knowing the meaning to life? Without a Women your structure or dynasty won't be complete. And that means that there is, no son or daughter that will leave an ounce of history behind! The Game should be ran with knowing the logical behavior of his mate and taking the time in thinking for her well being. One should love oneself before loving another! Why would any body love the other person more than himself, and why would a person want that person to love them more than he loves himself? See the Game doesn't allow the bullshit to get to you, it only makes it appear to be what it is, just bullshit! Sweet love or no love, regardless of what you do always maintain the logical way of thinking or you will suffer a heart break! The people of today are all confused and not thinking logical. There thinking in a system that makes the matrix looked planed. Money and fame rule them and confused their minds to believe that their purpose is to worship an idol. *"Love who you our, and not what makes you happy, the Game is good, but it can also be dirty."* Sometimes you have to know that your not the only person that's on earth. But, you are still the leader of the structure and have to maintain total Manhood. If not than your Kingdom will be up for grabs and Man will go extinct. You can't be seduce by words and sex and aspect to govern yourself in the proper manner. With dealing with the other person your Game has to be defined. You can't make the mistake, and not pay attention to what is real and to what is fake. People get toss in to something without thinking in the right mindset. They get caught loving but not getting loved. The only thing else is getting used. Unconditional love will leave you in a matter of seconds when dealing with negative people. When walking in a Kings path and trying to reach your total Man, your mind frame has to be logical and enlighten to others. Men, look at the people in your life and ask yourself, do they deserve to be loved! The caution to represent love is only logical. But, for some reason people don't use the common sense, and find themselves acting out of character. See the dog takes over and they find the leash is shorter than it has to be. To conquer love, the mind should know that you have to take a chance at it, and want to learn from it as well. Its only logical when you know the structure to be a successful King, that wants his Kingdom to be proud of him. The Game to this is to correct the wrong in the things you do! Without taking the time and learning your mate, is like abusing yourself. A Woman is complicated but with your boundaries and paying attention to detail, you can brake the attitude of complications. Any body who doesn't believe in love is a fool who's been beaten by it or a person who living off another person hurt. The only problem with love, is that some people use it for personal gain just to maintain the feeling of the idea of it. The individual who in it just for themselves makes more problems for their situation. The real reason love doesn't work is because Man and Women are to selfish with themselves to take part in it. Look, to make a strong Kingdom you have to give a little of yourself to get a lot of someone else. How do you think this society is ran, the people in charge of anything will give a little and get what they want! See that's why the bitch runs free, because the Men of today are living testament, to what is known as a bitch! Love & And Thinking Logical is base on a pimp's persona. Even a pimp catches a fraction of love when Choosing his bitches. The beauty of the Women is in her flesh. But, the essence of this creature is in her sprit. Why do we get roped into action, and then hang ourselves at the end?

The thinking process has to be logical so that you make the proper adjustments when dealing with another confused human being. Safe House issue the Game in moderation taking pieces of the Game and adding to your résumé. Men, it is better to be feared than love only because of circumstances. The utopia among the sexes is a fantasy that only exists in the minds of the individual. However, the individual is preoccupied with the fear of togetherness. So being cautious is the only choice when dealing with people with the same mindset. To be together, is what the creator design and is the only way to become Man. But the fear of the other person becomes a defense for them and they become stagnate. But it is logical to do this! The only problem would be that after years of the same old thing, that you become what they are, nothing! The bitch is the problem for your growth. Life expects you to take the journey towards marriage, but the bitch puts a damper on that type of relationship. Your zero tolerance to this animal is logical for this situation, but it seems that the Men of today is not thinking with their minds. So to love without thinking is very elementary. The Man can't think with that type of logic and be successful in seducing his love of his life. The only thing you will attract is what you are, a mind less and hart less human being! Everybody deserve love but only a few have the mindset to accomplish this dream. At Safe House we make dreams come true, this is based on your own decision making. Its not a bad idea to boost your Game to be able to vision the next stage of your life. Only a fool would refuse time, and not place himself in different era of his life. Ice burg Slim a pimp turn author, knew times were changing and he had to change his way of thinking so he could adapt to what was going on, in this modern day of pimping. The key thing you need to know is time! Time is your soul purpose for establishing your Manhood. You have to remember that time waits for no one. So Men, love And Think Logical when moving through life. Love the time you spend on earth and live logical while doing it, it would be the model for the gifted, who believe that the world is a crooked place and that, nothing seems to be what the world perceive it be. So not wanting or perusing love puts you in a situation where your in control of other people's fears of what love is. Now, having love is normal and only logical in dealing with human beings. However, people make choices and those choices lead them to not receive the gift that God granted them. The Game to love is always a challenge for the mind. But, beware of other people's minds, because everybody won't think in the manner of logic. You have to use your mind and muscle the thoughts of others, so you can delete their fantasy and show them a reality. If you don't put your Game down with perfection, your whole beginning can be your end. I knew this person who wanted love and all the things, that love itself could bring. But the gift to tell a lie, altered the perception of this individual. She wasn't thinking logical. From the beginning of anything, there is truth. For example if you buy something and it comes with instructions, you have to have the most truthful answers too question that you need answer when dealing with the product. If the instruction are not right the product will not work. So lying from beginning only delays the truth. The instruction she received were not from the creator. Her whole fight with love is one sided, and since she didn't know what love was or how to love, she found herself always looking for it! The Game see through the thick blind fold that, blinds people from seeing the truth. When being honest from the beginning, heighten their fears of what they really want. Leaving their actions not logical and confusing. With the Game that Safe House provides, Men can be fearless with life's problems with out any causality. So fear the truth! Why? You were put here for a reason, and that reason can steel be determine by you. The logic to love anything, has to be determine by you and only you. This is based on the individual and the mind, breaking apart from the masses and awaken to see the truth. Men, we have to see a greater purpose to create what God him self would want. If any of the teaching were correct, than lead your body to the brain and make the logical decision and start to live life!

CHAPTER 10

"THE STATE"

THE REASON WHY I wrote this section of book is because the world has too many enemies pushing people into their own mental slavery. The best thing to do is to cut the enemy off, before he or she get started. I bring you to the state! A self governing method that shows you how to conduct oneself while setting up a Safe House or a Kingdom, that can last for a 100 years or more. Your life should be presented in the fashion that you're a King and that your Kingdom should be protected at all times. Life in general is took for granted. Why do people abandon their circle of trust for choices that you don't make for the good of your own Kingdom? Why is it you pretend to position yourself that way, and why don't you take notice of what other people are trying to push on you? Rather, than think before you act, you take other people advice on how to live your life! My goal in this section is to show you how to create a state inside a state. They can't control your mind if their not in your life. The people that you love and respect have to be apart of a circle of trust, that has to be boxed in as tight as possible. The village of people can't be confused to not to obey the state. The state is you! It is depended on your way you rule. The essence of life is important to the Kingdom, so the way you live has to be thought out in a manner of success! There are rules and commandments to build a successful Kingdom. For one, you have to realize who you are, and you also have to have a proper understand of yourself worth! How can any form of the circle be completed if you don't believe in yourself. The next level in completing your task at hand is to realize that it can't be any other code but the one you choose! So many Men have been caught into what others are thinking of them, and forget how to think for themselves. People let other people dictate their life, and they find out how much respect that others have for them. Don't let anybody dictate your Kingdom! Once it is compromise your power will be divided and you will be overthrown. I have spent numerous amount of years study the masses and I came up with people are stupid and jealous and unforgiving. In my conclusion the world is filled with subjects and only one King. However, that's not true! That's what the people with the power want you to believe. During the time of Thomas Jefferson in a early draft of the Declaration of Independence Jefferson wrote the word *"Subject."* When he referred to the American public. He then erased that word and replaced it with *" Citizen."* A term used frequently throughout the final draft. The people in power misuse their position to control your Kingdom. With the Game that Safe House provides, a state can be built inside a state. But, being a subject will only hinder you from completing that task. You can't be a subject and a King at the same time, because the people won't believe in you! At Safe House a King is another form of a true Man. So lets analyze the person know as the subject or slave! This human being is like everybody else trapped into a society that say's that they care about you and your family but they really don't care about themselves. So how can they care about your Kingdom? These people are getting lead by an evil force that controls all their situation, without caring for one individual that's in society. However, it is possible to square off your perimeter and create your own Kingdom. Take position, and pull together your resources and take control of your Men and Women. Even if it's a boy or girl, make them see the picture before it becomes the painting!

" I have found that some people minds aren't developed to hold information that doesn't seems plausible, only information that's taught not found out. With this said, these people are nothing but mindless souls!" (Mindless Souls June From The World And Everything In It)

The quote that was presented, is what the world has to offer to all its subjects. To be a subject is to be a slave, and in slavery you do what ever the majority wants you to do! You never make your own decision. Your house should be ran with strict rule, so no Man can't separate what you create. You're the Mosses that runs your home! If you don't rule with the knowledge that the world isn't what they claimed it to be, than your Kingdom is doomed. And if you can't see people want to destroy your very existent, than your *"dead in the water"* as they might say! What, people don't understand is that God is the way. You can't ask another person for security because people are to selfish and not caring and for the simple fact they have their own life. The Game won't make sense to the individual if he not listen. God doesn't respect the one who doesn't listen, and if your not listen your not protecting your Kingdom. History has proven that race and gender has a lot to do with, if you get the right security. So why wait for another? Why not make your house a state! Can't you see the King of the subject is to blame for most of your problems. However, you can't blame them for your own decision to follow suit. Mindless souls trying to run a life that really doesn't exists, letting the King of the masses control the contents of their homes. The world doesn't have a clue on how you want to run your house hold. They only care about themselves, not what makes a family a unit. To their King, your just a social security number, standing in line waiting for welfare and food stamps. You don't have to have your hands out for help, because the help that your getting is from the same person that put you in this mess. Stop and think, how it was in the days of real Men. When Men could feel like their family was counting on him and not the King who lies to the people. Where does that leave your house hold, if this King is controlling your habitat? When a father was really a Man that governed his self to the value of his family. Now the system turn Men into what they fear the most *"A Male Bitch!"* The state is mandatory for your own survival the Game you use has to be thought out as if it is a blue print. One way in running the state is to maintain who you are at all times. The family should know you're the King of your world and that you have their interest in mind. Control the arm and the legs so you can move your army close together, in case your home is breeched. If you don't have everybody attention in your circle than the enemy will be right at your front door. The rest of the world will label you a schizophrenic and that may be so, to a person who doesn't know the Game. But why not look into the glass and see that there isn't any water in it. Why not see that empty promises is all they have to offer you and the family? What about the children and their children! How can a child respect you and call you father if your not in that position. The tactic of claming a state inside a state gives your children hope inside the belly of the beast. Rather than pushing them out to a world that wants them to fail. What does it take to reason with your logic? The people in the world do not care about you and your kids. However, you choose to deal with the enemy with open arms, you take yourself to doctors with the notion that they will help you when your sick. But the truth is that they are practicing medicine! Not a expert that the King of the mass want to portray on TV. But you let them into your life, trusting and obeying them at every will. Nothing safe anymore! Your playing Games with your life and your hurting the family's well being, when your not being what God created! Don't let the masses take away your birth rights to be King, and don't let somebody else run your Kingdom. So how can you trust these so called politician, doctors, pastors, lawyers and even your parents who been inducted into hall of fame of lies? When you don't even trust yourself. You pretend to offer yourself a life that doesn't even have a beginning rather than a middle or a end. What does it take for you to realize how much debt that you owe yourself for dealing with these people who work for the undertaker? You put yourself in a position that you are in by paying attention to mainstream logic, rather than your own! How can you abandon your principles for some one else's dreams. You can't think for yourself because you choose not to use your brain. The state puts you in the driving seat to take back your life. Remember with all hands on deck the opposition have no chance of in infiltrating your Kingdom. To keep your family structure together you have to keep the door close to advertisements that could lead an individual to break the law of your Kingdom. The state is apart of the Game that insure your family safety from people who run rabbit. Without it your family is unprotected and your Kingdom will be controlled by another that doesn't mean your family any good. So why let the King of the masses take what's rightly yours. How do we as human being believe in what ever they say? All through history we find this King to be more human than he appears to be. They change faces but remain devilish in decision that are made towards its people. The state should be properly guarded against this enemy.

"Again, the prince who holds a country differing in above respects ought to make himself the head and defender of his less powerful neighbors, and to weaken the more powerful amongst them, taking care that no foreigner as powerful as himself shall, by any accident, get a footing there; for it will always happen that such a one will be introduced by those who are discontented either through excess of ambition or through fear, as one has seen already. The Romans were brought into Greece by AEtolians and in every other country where they obtained a footing they were brought in by inhabitants. And the usual course of affairs is that, as soon as powerful foreigner enters a country, all the subjects states are drawn to him, moved by hatred which they feel against the ruling power. So that in respect those subjects states he has not to take any trouble to gain over to himself, for the whole of them quickly rally to the state which he has acquired there. He has only care that they do not get hold of too much power and to much authority, and then with his own forces, and with their goodwill, he can easily keep down the more powerful of them, so remain entirely master in the country. And he who does not properly manage this business will soon lose what he has acquired, and whilst he does hold it he will have endless difficulties and troubles."(Niccolo' Machiavelli From The Prince and Other Writings)

To understand what Mr. Machiavelli is saying, one

would have to see his life entirely only through his eyes, and also he would have to believe in what God created him for. When I look at the rest of the world it seems too understanding of the evil that's being place on them. When placing the outside world in your world or in other words your Kingdom, you leave secretes of your D.N.A. in plain sight. However, when I think of the Game, I picture a world where children can play and adults can be parents, and not subjects to a system that wishes for their participation in enslaving their mind and their body and their soul. These are the people who where made up individuals trying to be caring parents for hire! Waiting and watching for their child support checks, income tax check and any other check that they didn't earn. Why put yourself in a dilemma in which you will regret? You can't get caught up in this so called dream that the system has created for the masses. The dream is false, better yet its just imaginary! And only with a train eye can you catch the misfortune that comes with that dream. Bring your people out of the land that is oppressed. Like Mosses, lead the people out of the land of Egypt. Take and pack your bags and move your family into a hiding place. Make sure that the door is close behind you, and make it a point to tell the people that you will not break your convent with them. You cant have any traitors in your castle. If you do than the whole thing will come down brick by brick. I always wonder why a

Kingdom would fall from only one person. Where do you get the balls to follow a person that will lead you to your own separation of your circle. That's distasteful and disgusting! Why harm the hand that's feeding you and why put the house at risk for a hostile take over. The people should know their place in the state. If they do not, then the bricks will fall. Temptation to tell secretes will only leave your family tree in limbo. The Kingdom is the state and you are the Kingdom don't forget the position you were granted! Without you the army doesn't move, they only become trap in a reality of hating you! So how do you lose, if you create a state inside a state? The self protection method of separating, the world from your family or your family from the world, would benefit the mind from apposing enemies. The family has to know what to do when it comes to the Kingdom. Everybody has equal rights to what the state has to offer. But only one can lead and the rest is there for support. Without their support your standing alone with the wait of the world on your shoulders. Position, you and your family so all of you can feel stable inside the state. Safe House is what the state is all about! The Game that you put down to the family has to be resurrected from what God provided, when dealing with Man and Woman, So that the children could get tutored, to understand what position to play when the time comes for them to be adults. How can we blame the individual, who was never taught to take control of oneself , so that they can have the Holly Trinity! The State is what you should desire when dealing with the family that you keep. When you put a box around the circle of people that's in your life you begin to understand the matrix of what life has to offer. So you as the individual has to take control of your surroundings. The people in the box have to have the same understanding as yourself. They have to obey the state, they have to listen to the gospel that comes out your mouth! During a period in ancient Chinese history a Man by the name of *"Ts'ao Ts'ao that was such a strict disciplinarian that once, accordance with his own severe regulations against injury to standing crops, he condemned himself to death for having allowed his horse to stray into a field of corn! However, in lieu of losing his herd, he was persuaded to satisfy his sense of justice by cutting off his hair."*(James Clavell From Art of War)

"When you lay down a law, see that it is not disobeyed, the offender must be put to death." (Sun Tzu From The Art Of War)

The story Ts'ao Ts'ao, was meant to show the willingness of this Man, to present his loyalty of his Game. By being cautious with his herd or to punish himself for losing it, only shows reasonability for which he demanded from himself. To put in perspective, the disobeying of your wishes, leaves you the individual to put a death clause in the contract when dealing with another person. Cutting the individual from your presents, only enhances the state as a power. Dealing with this disobedient person will bring down the whole Kingdom. So to put to much effort into someone who doesn't want to believe in the state is a mistake waiting to happen! The bitch wants to become a problem for the Man, but only with option, can you deal with the hurt and the fear. The factor, when dealing with the bitch, is that you have to defused every situation with tactical methods no matter the cost! The picture with your chest out while holding your ground will send pulses of positive energy to the enemy, making them hurt and fearing what had just transpire. But brace yourself from the back lash! When check mate is in position redirect the bitch with another bold move, so that your constantly confusing the enemy. At Safe House the State is what is needed to protect the family structure from a individual who wants your Kingdom to fail. Creation, can only begin with Man and Women the rest is merely a scientific experiment! The bases to the State is to defend home at all cost. The Kingdom is your sanctuary, were you make important decisions on how to proceed in this criminal world. Your plains can't be spoiled, you have to place the structure in effect, so that the family knows their position. The disobedience of a individual will leave you and the family valuable to everything that's criminal. Children, significant other, and even you have to walk a life of enlightenment for the State to be effective in today's world.

" *You shall not make idols for yourselves; neither a carved image nor a sacred pillar shall you rear up for yourselves; nor shall you set up an engraved stone in your land, to bow down to it; for I am the Lord your God you shall keep my Sabbaths and reverence My sanctuary: I am the Lord. If you walk in my statutes and keep My commandments, and performed them, then I will give you rain in its seasons, the land shall yield its produce, and the trees of the field shall yield their fruit. Your threshing shall last till the time of vintage, and the vintage shall last till the time of sowing; you shall eat your bread to the full, and dwell in your land safely. I will give peace in the land, and shall lie down, and none will make you afraid; I will rid the land of evil beast, and the sword will not go through your land. You will chase your enemies, and they shall fall by the sword before you. Five of you shall chase a hundred, and a hundred of you shall put thousands to flight; your enemies shall fall by the sword before you. For I will look on you favorably and make fruitful, multiply you and confirm My convent with you. You shall eat the old harvest, and clear out the old because of the new. I will set My tabernacle among you, and My soul shall abhor you. I will walk among you and be your*

69

God, and you shall be My people. I am the Lord your God, who brought you out of the land of Egypt, that you should not be a slaves; I have broken the bands of your yoke and made you walk upright."(God- Blessing For Obedience Deut. 7 : 24-24; 28:1- 14 From The King James Bible)

"The State!"

CHAPTER 11

"THE WAR"

"If you know the enemy and yourself, you need not fear the result of a hundred battles. If you know yourself but not the enemy, for every victory gained you will suffer a defeat. If you know neither the enemy nor yourself, you will succumb in every battle...." (Sun Tzu The Art Of War)

THE WAR WITH ANYTHING will leave you tired and confused. Rather if it is a problem with a family member or a situation with a relationship or if its some kind of issue with race, you yourself have to realize the world is filled with deception and illusions. The war is not just against you, but everybody that's fighting the King of the masses. The people on his side are already brain washed looking for help and others are looking for favors. That leaves you and the people who believe in the Safe House methods of survival. The war with issues of self embodiment, leave the third eye to see the decision that you make are poor when dealing with oneself. Everything comes through you! It is true that evil exists, but the bitch can't get to you if you don't choose the life that the King of the masses has to offer. The strategies that move against you and your Kingdom are a means of destroying your inner self for the reason of controlling your mind. The dream only hinders you like slavery hinders the Man that picked the cotton. Like I said everything goes through you! The war, is your own war. Dealing with a relationship, the war of getting to know oneself puts you in a time machine. A gifted of being able to see the out come before it happens. The Game will lead your army, (that's your family) to what is profitable. The check list of your wants or better yet demands, leaves this situation in check mate, giving you the knowledge of oneself. How can you expect someone to know who you are and what you want! The demands have to be followed with strict measures. (That's your word!) How can your word be broken? The war between Man and Women is a identity problem. The mix signals and the confused state, leave you the individual at a stand still. Not achieving growth and a vision of a Kingdom. Can't you see the green pastures isn't so green! I guess marriage has its points! But a bitch in a form of a Woman clouds that plain. Most Men don't have the gift to see pre-existing behavior. They are too caught up into themselves to believe that the Woman he called the love of his life, could be possibly a bitch! The politics to Man and Woman leave Men weak and uneasy when dealing with the Woman. The war goes through you, you're the most important person in your life. The time is now! Take back your position, square off your perimeter and show your Manhood. The Woman was a gift from God, and you were created in his image, So that makes you Man! To present anything different to the opposite sex would be destroying to your character. The situation that you are in came from society! The war against you and people like you are crimes against humanity. The confusing thing is that there are as many Women that there are Men. However, the percentage of quality Man and Women are at a all time low. Due to society programming, and controlling affairs of the King, to steal the minds of the Women, leaving the bitch left standing with the sword in hand, fighting our battles raising our soldiers. It's sick to believe that God plain doesn't work. Man was created to lead, and Women to nurture and support the Kingdom. How did we get to were the world is today? Did we fail the Woman and push her to the King of the masses? The answer is yes, of course we did, with help from the enemy! During the time of 1712, a Man by the name of Willie Lynch came to America to produce a method in which to rule over a nation of people for numerous amount of years. It goes, that during those times, Africans were on hand, as test examples to the founding fathers. They took Man, Women, and children and broke them of everything, the foundation, the circle of trust! Just to get rid of the threat of the other Man. They took the image of Man and change it drastically and mangled and brutalize him in front of his Queen and his heir, leaving them to choose between life or death. So Women did have a reason, to be left to choose the enemy! But every war has it sense of death, but to choose the King of the masses over your child's father, leaves the father questioning the mothers loyalty to the Kingdom. It is true that the Woman is important for the survival of the people. So always remember the Game when dealing with the opposite sex. Your people need your Manhood! War is defined in Webster Dictionary to be," *To engage in warfare: be in conflict.*" Your life is in conflict! Everyday it's a fight to stay alive, even if your rich the war will test your mind. In this maze of confusion, the relationship brings deception and a illusion into your perception of what supposed to take place. Everything, comes through you!

The family member is hard to read just because

we were taught to believe that loyalty exists in the foundation. However, with the war that moves against your family structure, some individuals don't take notice to what the State has to offers, and proceed to run off course until the Kingdom is no more. Siblings will leave you in a tug of war from your fathers Kingdom to your Kingdom. Hate and jealousy fuel the conflict between brothers and sisters. Even though envy on your part leave the situation meaningless.

" Lord for give me for the anger that I feel today. Give me the strength to be a Man, to turn my check the other way. The Devil in the form of my enemy have tested me. Now I must retaliate before they get the best of me."(Eight Ball - Don't Come Around My Way track 2)

Mr. Eight ball had it right by the title of his album Lost! The track Don't Come Around My Way, leave the Siblings on the outside looking in. Siblings can't interfere with your Kingdom. Family can't be divided, the preparation to the blue print can't be argue about. The war at home won't help with the success of the Kingdom. It will only kill the family from with in. The art of destroying one's foundation is to start with what he loves the most. Like Mr. Lynch's theory in braking a slave, you take their children and kill their parents or better yet, you take their weak to destroy their strong! See its more to be a Man, than the average child knows! That's why the world is filled with people who are unaware of what position to play. Siblings has an end, just like it had a beginning. Your Kingdom will end with you and your siblings will keep moving until their lives is complete. My hope is that Safe House can provide resistant against the perpetrator who would put himself into your Kingdom. Family or foe, the mindset should awaken your common sense! You have to realize you're the most important person in your life. The illusion of a utopia is what the outside world sees. The State confirms and places Siblings into what we call at Safe House, a stable condition! The one who uses deception to deceive the Kingdom will only fail at life itself. The Game to war is to understand oneself in being involved in war itself! Family should not participate in wars against each other. The enemy wants to misinform the ugly duckling, so he can mold their minds against there reality.

The war against race is a pathetic one! With you being what race you our, you have to realize you are an individual, as well as a color. The system has been put in place to control the masses. What the masses posses is manual labor, an a idiot reasoning to what the King of the masses has inflicted on them. Its 2011 and beyond and race plays important part in the illusion of other people's wars. Does Mr. Lynch Have a point in his method of braking a slave? The enemy will only think of race in a manner of a distraction to a much bigger plain. Race is the illusion that distracts the mind from seeing the origin of the problems that you will face in life. The King of the masses will have you think that color controls your well being to your survival. But the truth is that surviving the color barrier is the least of your concerns. The people that surrounds your perimeter are not what they appear to be! What you see are individuals who been capture by the enemy. One can not be blinded by the illusion! For what he see's is what he see's, but to see one for who they our, and not who they seemed to be, is what is needed! Life without sprit is a life that can't be explain. Your race is not the definition of you! You are the race that you are. The King of the masses, just wants to dictate the mind to believe, matter is over mind! However, at Safe House our model is mind over matter. To fall short of anything, will leave you no closer to the finish line. The matter in this case is material, and the mind should suggest a purpose! The war between race should put you in the mindset of chess. Two different colors, at war! Family verse family, battling to the death. That's war! That is the war that's upon your door step. In every situation, war determines your fait. Your family should be your main concern. The idea of love for another human being is very important. So family can be full of different colors if they received the honor to be call family.

Their King created the hate to stop the individual from seeing the true plain at hand. Destroying your family, generation after generation. Were do you take a stand? When will you get it? The Game suggest, to take control of your logic and reasoning. Race is not a factor to the Game that Safe House places before you! To be a fool, too the King of the masses when dealing with race and family or just a relationship with another human being, always keep in mind that you love yourself! They teach you to hate the other person. Mr. Lynch spoke to people of James town saying, *"Don't forget you must pitch the Old Black Male vs. The Young Black and the Young Black Male against the Old Black Male. You must use the Dark Skin Slaves vs. The Light Skin Slaves and the Light Skin Slaves vs. the Dark Skin Slaves. You must use the Female vs. the Male and the Male vs. the Female. You must have your white servant and overseer Distrust all Blacks, but it is necessary that your slaves trust and depend on us. They must love, respect and trust only us."* (Willie Lynch - From The Willie Lynch Letter and The Making Of A Slave)

The King of the masses possess the theory of controlling a human being. The issue of race is the experiment to what Our Founding Fathers found that day on the banks of the James River. Their pursuit to power went through the Africans. Their total control over Americans left the dream seekers Under their spell and content in being a raciest to their brothers. So Mr. Lynch's theory of controlling the race card can effect your Manhood in the manner of running your state! Just like the Slaves of 1712, the picture of no Kingdom, no Woman, and no mind, leaves you the slave under a law that forbids you from being Man! If you can take a individual and brake him of everything, why would that individual trust him? Men find themselves at war with fantasy instead of reality! (The Game!)

CHAPTER 12

"WOMAN"

"Some times we stay looking for love in all the wrong places, spaces... races against time don't exist here. Just real Woman, sport channel and good beer! Follow me... to a zone were we can be alone... for real talk, a chill walk... along... some coast beside me in the midst of a gentle breeze, let your mind be at ease. Under palm trees... when they sway... the outside world is no longer part of your day. Dinner is served... reserved for just us with scented candles mounted in black sand, warm oil message from black Woman to black Man. Same in return... we learn... each other before we become lover, father, mother, other things come into play. Like spending a lazy day together hiding from cold weather. As I rest on your chest of the best lover I ever had... in a world... of words and picture perfect possibilities that

penetrate deep into the safe place of my mental space. She… is Woman… at peace we shall ever be. Relaxed in our conversation about long live life lesson, blessing and kisses that turn pages to create chapters that make harmony and laughter, happily ever after in a union of one plus one to make a son… to bear rings and a daughter to drop flowers at our feet and sing la, La, la melodies and purposely teach true meaning of us and happily tell stories about the birth of our babies, hold and kiss each other the way we… used to… forever fused through… heartbeat, voice, sound, kiss, touch and too much… to ever… be severed." (Woman - Janette Calhoun)

T HIS SECTION OF THE book is dedicated to Women who can teach their sons to notice the bitch and to teach their daughters not to be one! Who can explain it better than the person who wants and desire this lovely angel. Man and Woman are tied together like boats are to water. To keep the Kingdom in place you need each other for survival. Without one another the Game will not benefit you! Woman is the opposite of Man in the physical, but in the mental, as a individual, they are not so different. So the saying, "Men are from Mars and Women are from Venus", is not logical to the Game. It only gives you a reason to be separate and not functioning in the manner of togetherness. The Webster Dictionary, describes

Woman as: an adult female person, Woman kind, Feminine nature, Womanliness, A female servant or attendant. At Safe House, Woman is very important to the object of life it self. Our description of Woman is an adult female, a mother, a caregiver, a love of a Man's life. The situation doesn't change! The position can't change! The Game shows you what really exists in a real Woman. The illusion of today's Woman is not what the creator place on planet earth. Go to the text of any *"Good Book!"* See what the Gods have to say about the one called "Woman", and incorporate that with the Game that seems right for the situation. Real players make the right moves, like in chess! The energy that you present can only be combine with the right person. So try to understand your counter part. Woman, is what you want from your significant other. It can't be any other than what God created. Don't let the bitch confuse your sight of time! Woman is everything that you see, when dealing with the one that stands before you! Defuse the illusion so that the Woman can breath again! She's the mother of your children or soon to be! The Queen of your Kingdom, the love of your life. Give this person of interest, her rights to be in your circle. To understand that every move that you make is a move that benefits your Kingdom. The image of Woman is over shadowed by the bitch, making Men fear the Woman and not committing to his Kingdom. This angelic being,

"Woman" is the mother of all mothers. She's the child bearer of your seeds. A creator of all human life. (That's what God presented to the species!) Life without her is not a life at all. That's why, Safe House is determine to show you how importing it is to slay the bitch, with mental thinking! The Game is to understand what you want out of this person. If she performs her duties with lady like qualities, from the beginning, than she's half way through the process on what it takes to be Woman! See with all senses concentrated on the Woman in origin, you will be able to see what it is the bitch has to offer you! The Woman will show herself to you. She can only present herself off your presentation of yourself. It will only help the cause to be real as possible. She won't function under the spell of a perpetrator, she will only become what you hate the most. The Game of doing what's right for your Kingdom on both ends, will leave the family in a straight line towards freedom. Togetherness of Woman and Man is freedom from the fields of lust and lies. But to be Woman, a Man will never know! However, a Woman will create a window of hope for her seducer, so she can find his peace of mind. See if a person wants the other person to fail, than that person is not who they should be! Why do we shit on all Women, when we don't have too? Is sex all we want when dealing with this individual, or our we too stupid to see the bigger picture? Your job is to be able

to create an image that a Woman will find close to a father type, rather than her being a mother of a child that's over aged. You should, yourself present *"Man"* at the highest degree! What you will feel from this, is a holy presence of sprit that run through your body. To project this image of Man, you have to be real enough to find pleasure in doing what's right for the Kingdom. Ladies know the truth! The bitch knows your flaws. The Game to love a Woman and to protect her from herself, will only lead you to completeness in for filling the void that your mother left behind, when you be came of age. To do right for your Kingdom is to do right for yourself! The situation at hand, has to have a point! If the Creator, created Man and Woman to merge into parental parents, than that point of having each other is very important for Mankind and for the Man himself to recognize his Queen. The Man has to take back the thrown and become King! The Game to see the future can only be helpful in a mind of someone who wishes for the other person to progress! Your Woman understands this because it's the logical thing to believe in. At Safe House our belief is that the Woman is a Man's Earth, and without this planet our universe will not work, hell our solar system will crumble and Man will be no more! This gift from the creator is meant to teach others how to treat the Woman. Man learn this from there mothers, not from there fathers! The world is corrupt and full of bitches

Man and Women. However, the situation, of Woman and Man should be look at as just that! The world portrays, both parties as the definition in the Webster dictionary. But, you define yourself! The *"Game"* to the one called Woman, is to be *"Man"* and nothing else. My hope of your survival, in the mix of the war between the sexes, will lead you to Manhood! The *"Game"* and the *"Kingdom"* is *"You!"* Believe That you control your body and your decision making, even if it is very limited. The picture of the *"Woman,"* that Safe House present to you is a picture of our mothers as well as our daughters. There can't be nothing else! If so, you will get consumed by karma and they will become the monster that will destroy your Kingdom. To have this sight to distinguish between Woman or foe, is meant for your survival against the evil that surrounds you. The *"Game"* is only given to those who are chosen, to believe in a logical way of thinking!

"So to the Woman who can teach their son to notice the bitch, and to the one who can teach their daughters not to be the bitch and for the Woman to understand the option, that the bitch exists!" (June - Woman -The World - The World And Everything In It)

OUTRO:

EXODUS

"God and Nature first made us what we are, and then out of our own created genius we make ourselves what we want to be. Follow always that great law. Let the sky and God be our limit and Eternity our measurement."(Marcus Garvey 1887-1940)

"Everything has a end to it, and your mind should see the end before it happens. Life is for learning, and learning is want you will do! If you choose to accept the end than, from the beginning you will be planning for it." (Everything Has A End James Mickler- Safe House For Men)

REFERENCES:

SAFE HOUSE
"QUOTES"

TUPAC SHUAKUR
1. I Ain't Mad At You - From the album (All Eye's On Me)

EIGHT BALL
1. Bobby & Whitney - From the album (Pimp C Greatest Hits)
2. Don't Come Around My Way - From the album (Lost)
3. Set Up Shop - From the album (Dirty On Purpose)

TELA

1. Goldie The Griot - (Double Dose)

TOO SHORT
1. A Bitch Comes A Dime A Dozen - From the album (Gangster And Strippers)

WILLIE LYNCH
1. Making Of A Slave - From The book Making Of A Slave

BRUCE LEE
1. He Who Knows Not - From the internet

ABARHAM
1. That They Will Let Me Live - From the King James Bible

GOD
1. Blessing For Obedience From the King James Bible

RANDIE BLACKMON
1. Evaluate The One You Call Friends - From Person To Person

ROBERT GREEN
1. Art Of Seduction - From the book The Art Of Seduction

SAFE HOUSE

1. Without Man - From The Safe House Family

MARCUS GARVEY

1. God and Nature 1887-1940 - From The Internet

MIYAMOTO MUSASHI

1. You Win Battles 1584-1645 - From The Internet

AUTHOR'S LETTER

The books and the music that are used in reference, are not in anyway, used in a negative way towards the authors, that are being mention throughout this book, nor the cover. The gift of the Game is meant for the consumption of knowledge, so that it can be passed down to our sons, so they can become Kings!

www.ingramcontent.com/pod-product-compliance
Lightning Source LLC
Chambersburg PA
CBHW030402290526
45785CB00004B/1873